THE AMERICAN HOUSE
ARCHITECTURE COLORING BOOK

A. G. SMITH

DOVER PUBLICATIONS, INC.
MINEOLA, NEW YORK

A new addition to Dover's *Creative Haven* series for the experienced colorist, the thirty-one illustrations in this book showcase the rich and varied architecture of residential homes across the United States. Arranged chronologically, the detailed drawings range from the saltbox house of colonial times to the contemporary. Each drawing is accompanied by an informative caption and pages are perforated for easy removal and display.

Bibliographical Note

The American House Architecture Coloring Book, first published by Dover Publications, Inc., in 2016, contains a new selection of plates from *The American House Styles of Architecture Coloring Book* by A. G. Smith, originally published by Dover in 1983.

International Standard Book Number

ISBN-13: 978-0-486-80795-9
ISBN-10: 0-486-80795-9

Manufactured in the United States by RR Donnelley
80795901   2016
www.doverpublications.com

1. Saltbox House *(Jethro Coffin House, Nantucket, Massachusetts, ca. 1686).* The first English colonists in New England built one-room rectangular houses with a stone chimney on one end. The easiest way to add another room to an existing house was by the addition of a lean-to across the back. The house then took on the shape of a saltbox.

2. Hudson Valley Dutch (*Bries House, East Greenbush, New York, 1723*). Brick was the favorite building material of the early Dutch settlers in the Hudson Valley. The earliest Dutch houses had steep roofs with stepped gables. But by 1700 the gables were straight with one step or elbow at the lowest corners.

3. Maryland T-Plan House *(Otwell House, Oxford, Maryland, ca. 1730)*. Built by a planter of considerable means, this house consists of two rectangular structures joined to form a T.

4. German Stone House *(Hager's Fancy, Hagerstown, Maryland, 1740).*
The early German settlers of Pennsylvania and western Maryland found stone readily available for the construction of houses much like those they remembered from Bavaria or Moravia. The American versions retained much of their medieval flavor.

5. Georgian Transitional *(Cupola House, Edenton, North Carolina, 1758)*. The coastal region of North Carolina was a melting pot of Colonial architectural styles. This house combines New England, Virginian, and Georgian influences.

7. Philadelphia Georgian *(Mount Pleasant, Philadelphia, Pennsylvania, 1762).*
The most elaborate houses in the country were built in Philadelphia. Most
were of masonry construction and quite ambitious in scale. Mount Pleasant
was built of stone rubble covered with stucco to resemble finished stone.

8. Flemish Farmhouse *(Dyckman House, New York, New York, 1783)*. This house was originally a small bakehouse with a massive stone chimney. As its owner prospered, the house proper was built, incorporating the features of the locally prevailing Flemish tradition.

9. Log Cabin *(a surviving example from the southern Appalachian Mountains, North Carolina)*. For thousands of years the construction of shelters from logs had been a natural response to the heavily wooded environment of Northern Europe. When settlers from Northern Europe came to the American frontier, they brought their cabin-building techniques with them.

10. Louisiana Plantation House *(Homeplace Plantation, St. Charles Parish, Louisiana, ca. 1791).* The Homeplace Plantation is an example of the French raised-cottage tradition at its fullest development. The style evolved as a response to the hot, humid environment of the Bayou country. The main living area, raised above its often muddy surroundings, was able to catch any breeze that might be stirring.

11. Adam *(Cook-Oliver House, Salem, Mass achusetts, 1802)*. The Adam style, dominant during the Federal period, was named after its Scottish developer, the architect Robert Adam. Its principles were based on the study of Greek architecture.

12. Carpenter's Gothic (*Delamater House, Rhinebeck, New York, 1844*). Although their medieval European models were built of stone, many of the early Gothic Revival houses in America were built of wood—hence the term Carpenter's Gothic.

13. Half-Timbered House *(Moravian Cottage, Missouri, 1850).* Moravian pioneers from Pennsylvania and new immigrants to the American frontier from Germany held fast to their traditional way of building. Although it looks as if it belongs in the Black Forest in the Middle Ages, this house was actually built in the state of Missouri in the mid-nineteenth century.

15. Italian Villa *(Morse-Libby House, Portland, Maine, 1860).* Although originally based on the design of Italian farmhouses, the American Italianate villa could be quite grand. The façade was asymmetrical, and there was usually a tower to one side.

16. Moorish Revival *(Longwood, Natchez. Mississippi, 1860)*. The Victorian craze for revival architecture left few historic sources untouched. This elaborate fantasy, with its Moorish dome, windows, and detail was left unfinished with the beginning of the Civil War.

17. Second Empire *(cottage, Bangor, Maine, ca. 1870).* This style was very popular in France in the mid-nineteenth century, and its influence was soon felt across the Atlantic.

18. Victorian Gothic *(Earlville, New York, ca.1875).* This style combines all the elements of the earlier Gothic styles at once—the pointed Gothic windows, the Italianate tower, and a liberal application of ironwork. It also has the single most characteristic feature of the High Victorian Gothic Style—elaborate coloration.

19. Chateauesque *(Augustus Byram House, Chicago, Illinois, 1881).* This grand style was brought to America from France in the late 1860s, but did not fully develop until the 1880s. It is based on the Italian Renaissance and French Gothic traditions brought together during the reign of Francis I in the early sixteenth century.

20. Shingle *(Isaac Bell House, Newport, Rhode Island, 1883)*. The Shingle Style superseded the Queen Anne Style as the height of fashion in the 1880s. Although it has some features in common with the Queen Anne, it is much simpler in design.

21. Richardson Romanesque (*Ayer House, Chicago, Illinois, ca. 1885*). H. H. Richardson introduced the Romanesque Revival Style. As it was adopted by other architects (as in this house by Burnham and Root), it became known as Richardson Romanesque. It is identified by conical towers, rough stone surfaces, and often deeply recessed windows.

22. Queen Anne (*Hale House, Los Angeles, California, 1887*). The Queen Anne Style was popular in the United States from the late 1870s through the 1890s. Variety of form, color, texture, and materials distinguishes the style.

23. Art Nouveau (*Albert Sullivan House, Chicago, Illinois, 1892*). This modest row house was built by Louis Sulllivan, one of the country's greatest early-modern architects, for his brother. The geometric interlacing ornament is in the Art Nouveau tradition.

24. Sod House *(Oklahoma, 1894)*. When homesteaders settled on the Great Plains, they found very few trees for lumber. They therefore turned to the only material available—the prairie sod itself—to construct houses.

25. Prairie *(Frederick C. Robie House, Chicago, Illinois, 1909)*. This house, designed by Frank Lloyd Wright, is an advanced example of the Prairie Style. Wright advocated an "organic architecture" in which the house should be in complete harmony with its environment. The long lines of the Prairie house are intended to parallel the flatness of the Midwestern landscape.

26. Bungalow *(Los Angeles, California, 1910).* The bungalow, a type of small one-story house developed in California by the Greene brothers, is marked by its low roof and verandas. The example shown here is the Western Stick Style.

27. Pueblo (*Zimmerman House, Albuquerque, New Mexico, 1929*). The Pueblo Style is a regional revival style. It began in California at the turn of the century and soon spread throughout the Southwest. It is based upon the dwellings of the Pueblo Indians.

28. Spanish Colonial Revival *(Cravens House, Oklahoma City, Oklahoma, 1929).* The buildings of the early Spanish settlers in the Southwest were the inspiration for this revival. Low-pitched roofs with red tile are a hallmark of the Spanish Colonial house. To this style we owe the patio, so popular in today's suburban lifestyle.

29. International *(Marcel Breuer House, Lincoln, Massachusetts, 1939).* Houses in the International Style were designed from the inside out, the function of the interior spaces determining exterior form and appearance. This idea, originated by Frank Lloyd Wright, was soon incorporated into the principles of the Bauhaus School in Germany and further developed.

30. Miesian *(Philip Johnson Residence, New Canaan, Connecticut, 1949).* Known as the Glass House, the building was designed by architect Philip Johnson as his own residence. It is an excellent example of the Miesian Style which was developed by Ludwig Mies van der Rohe. It is based on the principles of skeletal construction, in which an exterior frame, rather than the walls themselves, support the structure.

31. Sustainable *(designed by John Milnes Baker, 1981)*. Sustainable architecture is a style that developed in the 1970s. Its goal is to lessen the negative environmental impact of homes and buildings by efficiency of construction and economy of operation. Prominent features of this style include solar panels, double-glazed windows, and natural materials.